IN AN EMERGENCY

Neil Champion

amicus

Published by Amicus
P.O. Box 1329
Mankato, MN 56002

Printed in the United States of America, at Corporate Graphics
in North Mankato, Minnesota.

Library of Congress Cataloging-in-Publication Data
Champion, Neil.
  In an emergency / by Neil Champion.
    p. cm. -- (Survive alive)
  Includes index.
  Summary: "Gives essential survival tips on what to do in emergency
situations. Includes scenarios about fire, bad weather, accidents, injuries,
extreme conditions, and more"--Provided by publisher.
  ISBN 978-1-60753-040-4 (library binding)
 1. Survival skills--Juvenile literature. I. Title.
  GF86.C44 2011
  613.6'9--dc22

Created by Appleseed Editions Ltd.
Designed and illustrated by Guy Callaby
Edited by Stephanie Turnbull
Picture research by Su Alexander

Picture credits:
l = left, r = right
Contents page Ashley Cooper/Alamy; 4 AfriPics.com/Alamy; 5l Jerry and Marcy
Monkman/EcoPhotography.com/Alamy, r Juniors Bildarchiv/Alamy; 6 LOOK Die
Bildagentur der Fotografen GmbH/Alamy; 7 Zig Urbanski/Alamy; 8 Harriet Cummings/
Alamy; 9 Arco Images GmbH/Alamy; 10 Peter Arnold, Inc/Alamy; 11 Alaska Stock LLC/
Alamy; 12 Pat & Chuck Blackley/Alamy; 13 Chris Gomersall/Alamy; 14 Realimage/Alamy;
15 Slanted Roof Studio/Alamy; 16 ColsMountains/Alamy; 17 Blickwinkel/Alamy; 18
AfriPics.com/Alamy; 19 Photoshot Holdings Ltd/Alamy; 20 Dennis Hallinan/Alamy; 21
Peter Arnold, Inc/Alamy; 22 Alaska Stock LLC/Alamy; 23 Ian Dagnall/Alamy; 24 Paul
Thompson Images/Alamy; 25 Chinju@Digipix/Alamy; 26 SHOUT/Alamy; 27 Ashley
Cooper/Alamy; 28 Juniors Bildarchiv/Alamy; 29l Photoshot Holdings Ltd/Alamy, r Alaska
Stock LLC/Alamy.

Front cover: Daniel H. Bailey/Corbis

DAD0038
22011

9 8 7 6 5 4 3 2

Contents

Disaster Strikes!

Imagine being caught in an Arctic blizzard, a desert sandstorm, or a jungle flood. Or how about coming face to face with an angry bear, a hungry crocodile, or a **venomous** snake? And what if you were stranded in the wilderness without water or lost in the mountains with no food? Would you know what to do?

All Kinds of Emergencies

Whether you're out for a short hike in the woods or heading off on an Arctic expedition, things can go wrong. The most common problems are minor injuries, such as cuts, bruises, and sprains, as well as getting lost and running out of food and water. Other problems depend on the terrain or the weather. For example, being exposed to freezing temperatures can cause **hypothermia**.

DID YOU KNOW?
*In an emergency situation, your body pumps **adrenaline** into your bloodstream to get you ready for action!*

If you're in the desert and see a huge, swirling sandstorm approaching, you should cover your face, lie down, and wait for the storm to pass.

Be Prepared

Whenever you head out into the wild, it's important to be prepared for any emergency. Always carry the right equipment and know how to use it. If you have good **survival** skills, you will be able to avoid or prevent a lot of problems—and you'll also know how to deal with anything unexpected that happens on the way.

▲ *Would you know what to do if a bear came nosing around your camp? Find lots of useful advice on page 19.*

Don't Panic!

Being prepared doesn't just mean carrying the right gear and learning useful skills. It also means having a positive attitude. Emergencies can be frightening and stressful. It's vital to stay calm and think clearly, or you may end up making your situation worse. Take a few deep breaths and deal with the most urgent problems first. It could make the difference between life and death!

▲ *Think hard about what you need to take and pack it all into a strong backpack. Make sure it isn't too heavy to carry!*

TRUE SURVIVAL STORY

JULIANE KOEPCKE was the only survivor of a plane crash deep in the Amazon rain forest in 1971. Koepcke, aged 17, kept calm and remembered what her father, a scientist, had told her about jungle survival—to follow a stream until it became a river, where there would be more chance of finding help. Koepcke found a stream and spent the next ten days wading, exhausted and hungry, through crocodile-infested waters. She had cuts on her arms that were soon crawling with maggots, but she kept going until she came to a hut. The next day, a group of lumberjacks found her there and took her to safety.

Using Your Head

It isn't always easy to get help for an emergency in the wild. Even if you are able to contact someone, it could be hours, or even days, before they reach you. It's up to you to survive—so you need to be smart, organized, and sensible. Here are some vital tips for coping with emergency situations.

Do Your Homework

Good planning from home can help you avoid bad situations. Research the area you are visiting before you set off. Look carefully at a map to see if there are any dangerous features, such as steep cliffs or large rivers that could flood. Check the weather forecast. Are storms or hurricanes predicted? Is it a hot, dry time of year when forest fires could start, and is there a strong wind that would fan the flames?

▲ *If you'll be climbing steep rocks, take the right equipment. Go with a guide and don't attempt anything you're not comfortable with.*

Take a Survival Kit

Whenever you go into the wild, take small, essential items such as a knife, rope, matches, a compass, safety pins, and a candle. They may come in handy in an emergency. However, you should also learn to manage without these things, just in case you lose them!

Learn Basic Skills

You can't plan for every emergency, but you can learn how to deal with them. Taking a first aid course could be very useful. It's also important to know how to read a map and use a compass (see page 15).

*Know how to build a good fire. Light **tinder** first, then prop larger sticks around the fire in a pyramid shape.*

*Learn to make shelters out of a **tarpaulin**. Make a tent between two trees like this...*

...or weigh down the material at each end like this.

▲ *Rock falls like this one often happen in steep valleys. They can start an avalanche of bigger rocks, so watch out.*

Stop, Think, and Plan

Whatever happens in the wild, remember that safety comes first. For example, if rocks fall from a cliff and hurt a friend, don't run straight over to help. Stop and wait to see if more rocks are about to fall. Once you're sure it's safe, go and assess how injured your friend is. Next, make a plan of action. If your friend isn't badly hurt, think how you can move him to safer ground. If he is badly injured, then you must get medical help.

First Aid Skills

Even if you're very careful, you may sometimes get minor injuries such as cuts, scrapes, or blisters. These are usually easy to deal with if you know basic first aid. The important thing is to take action quickly to prevent an injury from getting worse. For example, a cut can become infected if you don't clean and dress it.

It's useful to carry a small first aid kit with you whenever you set out on a trip.

Treating a Wound

This is how you should treat a cut, scrape, or other small wound.

1. *First, remove any dirt or splinters from the wound. Then clean the area carefully. You need fresh water and **antiseptic** wipes to do this properly. Dry the wound by gently dabbing it with a clean cloth.*

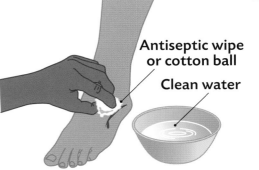

Antiseptic wipe or cotton ball

Clean water

2. *If the wound is bleeding, put a **gauze** pad or other clean, absorbent material on top and hold it firmly in place. You may have to use several pads before the bleeding stops.*

3. *Next, dress the wound. This means putting on a bandage or other **sterile** covering that will keep the wound clean and help it heal.*

ARON RALSTON was climbing in Utah, in 2003, when a huge boulder fell and pinned his right arm to the rock wall. He spent five days trying desperately to move the boulder, but with no luck. Soon his water supplies were gone. He had no cell phone and hadn't told anyone his plans, so he knew no one would be looking for him. Desperate, he decided to take serious action. Using a blunt pocketknife, he hacked off his arm just below the elbow. He then managed to climb down steep rocks to the ground and kept walking until he met a family out hiking, who gave him food and water and called for help.

Blisters

Blisters are swellings that are caused by something rubbing against your skin, usually on your feet. Try to avoid them by wearing comfortable footwear and good socks. To treat a blister, cushion it with a bandage. Don't prick it unless you have a **sterilized** needle and sterile dressing.

Natural Remedies

You can also use plants to help soothe and heal minor injuries. Common plantain is a weed that helps stop bleeding. Crush the leaves to a pulp and put them on the wound. Hold them in place with a strip of material or long grass. Moss is also useful for controlling bleeding.

Moss pressed onto wound

DID YOU KNOW?
Some mosses, such as sphagnum moss, are mildly antiseptic, which makes them ideal for using as pads or dressings on small wounds.

◄ *Common plantain leaves can also ease insect or nettle stings and soothe burns.*

Extreme Cold

Becoming too cold can lead to serious problems. If you're exposed to low temperatures and bad weather—for example, in mountains or polar regions—then serious conditions such as hypothermia and **frostbite** are real risks. You must be able to recognize the signs of these conditions and know how to treat them. If not, they could be fatal.

These Inuit children in Alaska are wearing traditional fur parkas that protect them from the icy wind.

TRUE SURVIVAL STORY

JIM BAILEY AND JESSE GRAY were hunting guides in Alaska. At the end of the season, the two men set off for home in their tiny aircraft, but got caught in thick fog and heavy snow and crashed into the icy Bering Sea. Numb with cold and shock, they managed to swim ashore and huddled together on the beach, shaking uncontrollably from hypothermia. They realized their only chance of survival was to keep moving, so they began to stagger along, stumbling from cramps and tiredness. Two days later, a small aircraft flew by overhead. Fortunately, the pilot saw Bailey and Gray below and picked them up.

Take Action!

If you spot early signs of hypothermia in someone, act quickly to prevent it from getting worse.

1. *Stop what you're doing and get everyone out of the cold. Shelter close together in a tent, cave, or other small space so you can share each other's heat.*

2. *Give the cold person warm clothes and a sleeping bag or blankets. Make sure he has warm drinks and food. He should soon feel better.*

Wind and Rain

The combination of wind and rain can be deadly. If part of your body is exposed to wind and rain, it loses heat about 20 times faster than normal. Once this happens, it's hard to stop from getting even colder, and hypothermia can set in. If you're exposed to the cold for a long time, parts of your body such as your nose, ears, hands, and feet can become frostbitten.

Spot the Signs

Try to avoid hypothermia by wearing warm clothing, keeping active, and taking shelter in bad weather. If people start behaving unusually—for example, becoming very quiet and cutting themselves off from others—then they may have hypothermia. They might also slur their speech or start shivering.

▼ *If you're out in the cold for a long time, like this Arctic sled driver, moisture from your breath freezes on your face.*

Extreme Heat

Heat can be as deadly as the cold. In very hot conditions, your body can become overheated and **dehydrated**. If you don't act quickly to treat these conditions, you may collapse and even die. Learn to spot the signs of heat-related problems before they become emergencies.

▲ In hot places such as this desert in Arizona, your body loses lots of water because you sweat so much. It's vital to drink plenty of water to replace these fluids and keep your body working properly.

DID YOU KNOW?
As you sweat, your body loses salt as well as water. This is why people who are dehydrated are given salty water, called saline, in the hospital.

Heat Exhaustion

If you're working hard, for example, climbing a steep hill with a large backpack, your body may lose so much water through sweating and heavy breathing that you start feeling very tired, thirsty, and dizzy. This is called heat exhaustion. It can happen even faster on a hot day. You may also have a fast heartbeat and a high temperature. You must get out of the sun, rest, and drink plenty of water.

TRUE SURVIVAL STORY

CHARLES STURT set off from Adelaide in 1844 to explore central Australia. What he discovered was a vast, fiercely hot desert. There was also a **drought**, so the land was especially barren. He, his men, and their horses suffered horribly as they trudged over endless sand dunes, with no shelter from the baking heat. They were dehydrated, starving, and ill, and their skin was cracked and sore from the blowing sand. It was so hot their thermometers burst. Finally, they gave up and hiked back to Adelaide.

Heatstroke

If heat exhaustion is left untreated, it can lead to a serious condition called heatstroke, or sunstroke. As your temperature keeps rising, your body stops working properly and you feel confused and faint. You may lose so much water that you stop sweating altogether.

1. *If someone has heatstroke, get him out of the sun at once and try to bring down his body temperature.*

2. *Place cold, wet towels on him and fan the air around him to make it cooler. You also need medical help. See pages 26 and 27 for advice on how to get help. If you act quickly, the person will probably survive.*

Keep Cool

To avoid heat problems, try not to be too energetic during the day. Travel in the early morning, evening, or even at night when the air is cooler, and rest in the shade in the daytime. There may not be much shade in the desert, so look for trees, caves, or rocky outcrops, or rig up a shelter using a blanket or clothing. Sip water throughout the day so you don't get too dehydrated.

▶ *Many animals avoid hot sun, too. Here, African springboks rest under a tree.*

Lost!

When you're in unknown terrain, it's very important to take a map and keep checking it to make sure you know where you are. But if you do get lost, don't panic! Stop walking, stay calm, and try to think clearly about where you are. Here are some tips for finding your way again.

Memory Test

Think what the land has been like for the last half hour of walking. Have you gone uphill, downhill, or across a river? Try to remember where you were when you last knew your location. Find it on the map and see if you can use it to figure out where you are now.

If the weather is foggy, or if a sudden blizzard blows up, it can be easy to get confused and lost.

TRUE SURVIVAL STORY

MARY O'BRIEN set off on a hiking trip in the mountains of Washington state in 2007. Heavy snow obscured the trail and O'Brien didn't have a good map, but she kept going and climbed much farther than she'd planned. Then she missed a vital turn. Soon night fell, and she was completely lost. She spent five terrifying days in rugged mountain terrain, hacking through dense, spiky undergrowth and stumbling across dangerous, crumbling rocks. At last, exhausted, she reached a river and was spotted by people in a boat.

Use Your Eyes

As well as using your memory, you also need to look around you carefully. What large or distinctive features can you see— a hill, a lake, a forest, or paths? If you have a map, try to find these features. Can you now figure out where you are in relation to them? Find all the clues you can and try to piece them together.

Find a high place to look around for landmarks. Using binoculars makes this easier.

DID YOU KNOW?
If the sun is shining, you can use it to help figure out which direction you're facing. The sun always rises in the east and sets in the west.

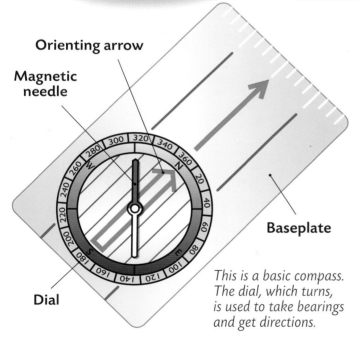

Orienting arrow

Magnetic needle

Baseplate

Dial

This is a basic compass. The dial, which turns, is used to take bearings and get directions.

Using a Compass

A compass is an essential tool in the wild. The red half of the compass needle always points north, because it is magnetic and is pulled toward the Earth's **magnetic North Pole**. Once you know which way is north, you can work out which way is south, east, and west. You can also use your compass with a map to take a **bearing**.

Explore the Land

If you have a compass, you can use it to explore your surroundings without wandering even farther off course.

1. *Put a clearly visible object on the ground. This is your starting point. Now take a bearing north and walk about 100 paces. What do you see?*

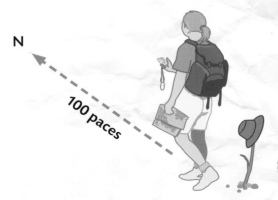

N

100 paces

2. *Take a bearing to your starting point and go back. Now take a bearing west, then east and south. As you build up a picture of the land, try to fit it to the map.*

Dangerous Places

There are all kinds of hazards in the wilderness. You may encounter crumbling cliffs, raging rivers, dense jungles, or treacherous swamps. Consider these obstacles when planning your trip, and be prepared for problems such as rock falls, landslides, and avalanches.

Watch Your Footing

Always be careful when climbing up or down steep rocks. Think about what would happen if you slipped. If you'd just slide a small distance, then continue. If you'd fall a long way, then stop. You must either turn back or find another route. Never attempt to climb up or down sheer cliff faces.

DID YOU KNOW?
Your shelter could be the most dangerous place of all, if it doesn't have enough **ventilation**. **Carbon dioxide** *can build up to a dangerously high level in an enclosed space.*

▼ *These hikers are on scrambling terrain, which means they have to use their hands to help them clamber up the rocks.*

Avalanche!

Avalanches are masses of loose snow or huge slabs of packed snow that slide rapidly down mountainsides. Avalanches can occur when lots of snow falls, or after a change in wind direction, or when the temperature rises and snow heats up. Help avoid them by traveling with an experienced guide and paying attention to avalanche warnings.

▶ *A team of mountain rescuers in France searches for avalanche victims.*

Escaping Quicksand

On riverbanks, in marshes, or near the sea you may find areas of oozing, wet sand called quicksand that can suck you in. If this happens, don't struggle or you will sink deeper. Lie flat on your back or stomach so that your weight is evenly spread over a large area. Slowly move across to drier land.

Quicksand isn't usually very deep, but it can be hard to get out of. Lie like this to avoid sinking.

Steamy Swamps

It's very difficult to travel through jungle swamps, either by boat or on foot. The water is often deep, **stagnant**, and clogged with masses of tangled roots. To avoid getting lost in the maze of winding water routes, you need a good map or—even better—a local guide to show you the way.

Crossing Rivers

Cross rivers at a bridge, even if it means going out of your way to find one. If there is no bridge and you really have to get across, find a stretch of water that is shallow enough to wade through. Wide sections are usually less deep, with a weaker current. Beware: rivers rise quickly in heavy rain or when snow is melting. If in doubt, turn back!

1. *Cross the river diagonally, in the direction the water is flowing, so you won't have to fight against the current.*

2. *Try using a pole for support. Don't put your weight on it until you're sure it's stable, or you could fall. Drag your feet, don't lift them, or you could lose your balance.*

Don't use logs or rocks as stepping stones, as they may be slippery. Only cross a river with an experienced adult, and as a last resort.

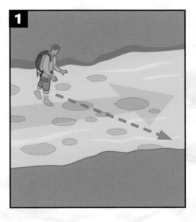

Angry Animals

Wild animals can be extremely dangerous. Bears and crocodiles could kill you in an attack, snakes can bite, and some insects carry nasty diseases. The most important thing to remember is that most animals don't want anything to do with you. They will usually only attack if they feel threatened. If you respect their habitat and stay at a safe distance, you greatly reduce your chances of getting hurt.

▼ *A scorpion in Botswana raises the venomous hook on the end of its tail, ready to sting.*

DID YOU KNOW?
Some people have a severe allergic reaction to insect bites and stings. This is called anaphylactic shock and needs urgent medical treatment.

Be Bear Aware

In bear territory, you can avoid disturbing bears by sticking to paths, hiking in a group, and camping in open areas. If you see a bear in the distance, move away slowly. Most problems occur when thoughtless campers feed bears or leave food lying around, so bears lose their natural fear of people and start coming to campsites in search of food.

If a bear comes near your camp, make lots of noise, such as shouting and banging pans, to scare it away. Don't turn and run, as bears are very fast runners. Climbing a tree is also a bad idea as **grizzly bears** can climb well.

Bears have a good sense of smell, so store food and anything smelly in sealed bags. Hang them out of reach.

Snake Bites

Always try to avoid disturbing snakes. Stay clear of piles of rocks or logs, as snakes like to shelter there, and wear long pants and heavy boots to protect your legs. All snakes can bite, but venomous snakes have two fangs that leave large, painful puncture marks in skin. If a venomous snake bites you, wash the area with soap and water and get help fast. Never put ice on the bite or cut the skin to get rid of the venom.

▲ *A rattlesnake raises its head to bite, revealing its large, venomous fangs.*

Small, But Deadly

Some insects can be very dangerous. For example, mosquitoes can transmit diseases such as **malaria** through bites. This means that you should always use insect repellent, wear long pants and sleeves, and sleep under mosquito nets. Watch out for ticks, too. They dig into your skin and can pass on **Lyme disease**. You can remove them with tweezers or special tick removers.

TRUE SURVIVAL STORY

NELL AND JIM HAMM are a retired couple who were out in a state park in California, in 2007, when a cougar unexpectedly pounced on Jim and grabbed his head in its jaws. Nell picked up a log and swung it at the animal, trying to make it let go. The animal then turned on Nell and crouched, ready to pounce. Nell screamed and waved the log in the air to make herself look bigger and more threatening. Luckily, it worked. The cougar retreated, and Nell helped Jim walk to a road, where she flagged down a car and got help. Jim later recovered in the hospital. This just shows how important it is not to hike alone!

Wild Weather

Severe weather causes all kinds of emergencies. Strong winds, thick fog, and torrential rain can make you lose your way or your footing. Heavy snow can cause deadly **whiteouts**, and lightning strikes can injure or kill you. If you're heading into the wilderness, you must plan and prepare for all kinds of weather conditions.

Check the Forecast

Get as much weather information as you can before you go. Look at long-range forecasts and pay attention to weather warnings. Bear in mind that strong winds can blow in bad weather sooner than forecasters predicted, and be prepared to delay or call off your expedition if weather is too severe.

▼ *Lightning flashes fill the sky during a tropical storm in South America.*

An enormous, violent tornado rips through fields in South Dakota.

Whirling Wind

Huge, swirling columns of wind called tornadoes can race along at speeds of more than 300 miles (480 km) per hour, ripping up trees and flinging debris into the air. If you find yourself in a tornado's path, shelter in a building, preferably in a basement, away from windows. If you're out in the open, crouch down on the lowest ground you can find, away from large objects such as trees that may be blown onto you.

Brace yourself in this position if you're caught in a tornado's path.

Flash Floods

Heavy rain can cause rivers and lakes to burst their banks and flood low-lying areas nearby. In very dry places, such as deserts, a lot of rain creates instant rivers that gush through narrow **gorges**. Always camp on high ground, away from rivers, and don't walk in gorges that would be hard to climb out of quickly.

Lightning

Lightning tends to strike the tallest point in the area, so if you're caught in a storm, never shelter under trees or other tall structures. Get down from hills or mountain ridges as quickly and safely as possible, and crouch as low as you can. Electricity from lightning can also travel through the ground, so sit on your backpack to provide **insulation**. Stay away from metal, stone, and water, as they all **conduct** lightning well.

In a storm, sheltering in a small cave can be dangerous. If lightning hits the cave roof, electrical currents may flow through the rock, jump across the gap, and reach you below.

Fire!

Fire is one of nature's biggest hazards. Some forest fires start naturally when there is a lot of dry debris on the ground. Others are sparked by lightning strikes, or begun by hikers who are careless with matches. Fires can spread incredibly quickly, especially in dry weather and when there is a strong wind.

Fire Types

There are three main types of fire. Ground fires burn in the soil just below the surface. They can smolder for months, killing plant and tree roots, then burst into flame if a gust of wind gives them more **oxygen** to burn. Surface fires race through undergrowth. Crown fires spread rapidly through the treetops, quickly engulfing huge areas of forest.

Warning Signs

Learn to spot early signs of forest fires. First, animals behave strangely—birds seem agitated, small animals such as rabbits disappear underground, and larger animals such as deer may start running away. Next, you will smell smoke from the fire.

▼ *This fire in Alaska devastated a wildlife refuge. Big forest fires can do serious harm to animals, birds, and the landscape.*

DID YOU KNOW?

Never jump into a pond to avoid an approaching fire. The water will heat up as the fire burns all around and you'll be scalded.

Buried Alive!

If you were caught in a forest fire, it might be possible to bury yourself in dry ground and survive. The soil would shield you from the worst of the heat. However, it's a risky strategy as you could be badly burned. Also, as the fire burned around you, it would use up the oxygen from the air, leaving you unable to breathe.

▲ *Seeds in the ground will soon sprout after a fire, but it can take many years for the area to recover.*

What to Do

A forest fire can move very fast, so don't try to outrun it. Instead, go around the fire if possible and away from the direction the wind is blowing. Don't move to higher ground—fire spreads quickly uphill as the heat rises and ignites fuel higher up. Aim for clear, open areas of low ground.

If a fire starts, the best place to be is on low ground, downwind of the fire. Don't get trapped in caves or in water.

Campfire Safety

Make sure you never start a forest fire. If you're making a campfire, choose a clear, open area with no overhanging trees that could catch fire. Keep the fire small, and watch it at all times. Never leave the site until you're sure the fire is completely out. Fires can spread underground through smoldering tree roots, so check that the ground nearby isn't hot or smoking.

*Always rake over the remains of a campfire to help **embers** cool. Make sure you turn over large stones.*

Pour cold water over the ashes, rake them again, and then scatter them.

Hunger and Thirst

Running out of food and water in the wild can be a big problem. You could only live for three or four days without water—and this survival time is even shorter in hot places. You could survive for seven days or more without food, but you would be very weak. Being able to find supplies in the wild is a key survival skill.

Running Water

If you need drinking water, look for fast-moving streams or rivers. Flowing water is far more likely to be safe for drinking than still water. This is because **bacteria** can't grow as easily in flowing water. Always walk upstream as far as you can to check that nothing has fallen in the water that could **pollute** it, such as a dead animal.

◀ *Look for clear, gushing water like this rather than pools, where water may be stagnant.*

Collecting Water

If you can't see a river or stream, then you need to find water another way. Catch rain in cups, or use one of these methods.

1. *Leave a metal dish out overnight. In the morning, mop up the dew that has formed on it.*

Pulp

2. *In a desert, cut open a barrel cactus, scoop out the pulp, and squeeze water from it.*

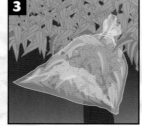

3. *In a jungle, tie a plastic bag over non-poisonous leaves. Water will **evaporate** from the leaves and then **condense** in the bag.*

TRUE SURVIVAL STORY

DEREK MAMOYAC set off to climb Mount Adams in Washington in 2008. Close to the summit, Mamoyac slipped and fell a long way. He was left with a broken ankle and couldn't walk, so he had to drag himself down the mountain. He had a few cereal bars with him and one bottle of water, but they only lasted a few days. He drank water from a stream and ate berries, but it wasn't enough, so he tried ants, centipedes, and even a large spider. It wasn't pleasant, but it helped keep him alive until rescuers finally found him!

Cleaning Water

You should always clean water from natural sources, as this kills harmful bacteria and gets rid of any pollution. The simplest way is to boil it for at least ten minutes. You can also filter it through a clean sock or other cloth to remove small pieces of grit, dirt, and other debris.

Many hikers carry lightweight stoves for boiling water and cooking. Stoves use fuel such as gas.

Finding Food

You can find food in all kinds of wild places, but you need to know what to look for. In mild climates, there are many edible fruits, seeds, and nuts, plus weeds, such as nettles and dandelions. If you're by the sea, try boiling seaweed. In the Arctic, you can eat some mosses and **lichens**. There is even food in deserts, including dates, gourds, and prickly pears.

Beware!

Not all plants are edible. Some may make you feel ill and others are so deadly they can kill you. Avoid unfamiliar red plants and berries since they are often poisonous, and don't eat plants with milky sap. Learn to identify poisonous plants before you go into the wild, and never eat an unknown plant. It's better to be hungry than poisoned!

◀ *The hard, shiny, red seeds of this tropical rosary pea plant are very **toxic**. Eating just one seed could kill you.*

Getting Help

When you've done everything you possibly can in an emergency situation but you're still in trouble, it's time to get expert help. Many countries have excellent emergency services that use helicopters, boats, and other vehicles to reach people who are injured or lost in remote places. But unless you have a phone, how do you contact them?

▼ *A rescue helicopter in the Tatra Mountains, Poland, arrives to lift a climber to safety.*

DID YOU KNOW?
Making three fires in a triangle is an internationally recognized sign that help is needed.

Here I Am!

You can try to attract the attention of rescue aircraft by making large signs on the ground with sticks, rocks, or brightly colored materials. Choose open areas, as high up as possible. On a sunny day, you might also be able to reflect sunlight off a mirror.

1

1. *In daylight, make a smoke signal by building a log frame and lighting a fire inside.*

2. *Pile evergreen boughs on the frame. They will produce lots of smoke as the fire burns.*

2

*A **signal flare** is another way of attracting help in the wilderness.*

Rescue Tips

If you see a rescue helicopter above, don't wave frantically. The pilot may think you mean it's dangerous to land. Stretch out both arms to show you need picking up. Make sure that you move backpacks and any other gear from the area where the aircraft will land, as the draft from the rotor blades will send nearby objects flying into the air. At night, don't shine a torch directly at the aircraft as it will obstruct the pilot's vision.

Holding your arms straight up tells the pilot you want to be picked up.

Distress Signals

If there may be people nearby, try shouting for help. If not, make this distress signal, which is used worldwide.

1. *Blow six blasts on a whistle or make six flashes with a flashlight. Wait for one minute, then make six more signals. Keep doing it until you get a response.*

2. *If you hear three whistle blasts or see three flashes in return, then you know help is on its way.*

Moving your arms slowly up and down tells the pilot to descend.

Test Your Survival Skills

Are you ready to deal with emergency situations in the wilderness?
Do you have the skills and sense you need to survive?
Take this quiz and find out! The answers are on page 32.

1. In an emergency, the most important thing is to...
a) Keep moving.
b) Shout as loudly as you can.
c) Stay calm.
d) Do nothing and wait for help.

2. Why is it a good idea to sit on your backpack in a storm?
a) It stops you from getting struck by electrical currents in the ground.
b) It keeps you from getting cold.
c) It stops your things from being blown away.
d) It stops you from getting struck by lightning from above.

3. Where is the best place to shelter from this storm?
a) On low, marshy ground   b) Under the tree
c) In the valley   d) In the cave

4. Which of these is NOT a good way of treating hypothermia?
a) Finding shelter.
b) Keeping still.
c) Having a hot drink.
d) Getting into a sleeping bag.

5. There's a bear in your campsite! What do you do?
a) Run away.
b) Climb a tall tree.
c) Try to fight him.
d) Make lots of noise to scare him away.

6. Why is it a bad idea to walk through a steep desert gorge?
a) It's too hot there.
b) The ground is very uneven.
c) It could flood quickly in bad weather.
d) The path is too narrow.

7. If your body loses a lot of water, you will begin to suffer from...
a) Malaria
b) Dehydration
c) Anaphylactic shock
d) Lyme disease

8. You're on a hill and see a forest fire in the valley behind you. It's spreading your way fast. What should you do?
a) Nothing—you're safe up the hill.
b) Go downhill and around the fire.
c) Crouch in a cave until it passes.
d) Wade into a stream so flames can't reach you.

9. Which of these snake facts is false?
a) Only venomous snakes will bite you.
b) Snakes like to hide in shady places.
c) Venomous snakes have two large fangs.
d) To treat a snake bite, wash the area with soap and water and get help.

10. What can be crushed and put on wounds to help stop them from bleeding?
a) Barrel cactus pulp
b) Rosary pea seeds
c) Boiled seaweed
d) Common plantain leaves

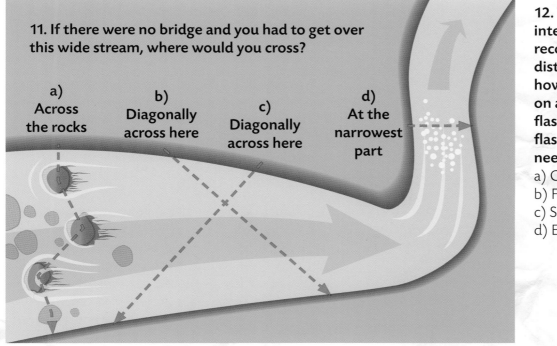

11. If there were no bridge and you had to get over this wide stream, where would you cross?

a)
Across the rocks

b)
Diagonally across here

c)
Diagonally across here

d)
At the narrowest part

12. To create an internationally recognized distress signal, how many blasts on a whistle or flashes with a flashlight do you need to make?
a) One
b) Four
c) Six
d) Eight

Glossary

adrenaline   A chemical substance that is produced in the body in response to stress.

antiseptic   A substance that destroys disease-causing bacteria or stops them from growing.

bacteria   Tiny, single-celled living things. Some are harmless, but others can cause diseases.

bearing   The direction you need to go in, measured from a known position.

carbon dioxide   A gas in the air. You make carbon dioxide in your body and get rid of it when you breathe out. In small, unventilated areas, carbon dioxide can build up to a very high level. This causes drowsiness and could eventually make you lose consciousness.

condense   To change from a gas or vapor into liquid. Water evaporates from plants as vapor and condenses into water droplets as it cools.

conduct   To transmit electricity or heat.

dehydrated   Suffering from loss of water from your body. It is dangerous to become too dehydrated because your body cannot work properly without water. Take regular sips of water to avoid dehydration.

drought   A long period in which there is very little rainfall. Droughts can last for months or even years.

ember   A glowing, hot fragment of wood or other fuel, left when a fire has burned down.

evaporate   To change from a liquid or solid to a gas or vapor. Water inside plants evaporates through leaves when it heats up.

frostbite   A painful condition in which skin and other tissue in the body is damaged because of extreme cold. It usually affects extremities such as hands and feet, as these parts get colder sooner than the rest of the body.

gauze   A type of fine cotton cloth used for bandages and other dressings.

gorge   A deep valley between cliffs, often carved out over many years by a river. Another word for a gorge is a canyon.

GPS receiver   A device that picks up signals from satellites in space and uses them to calculate its exact position on the Earth's surface. GPS stands for Global Positioning System.

grizzly bear   A type of brown bear that usually lives in western North America. Grizzlies can be extremely aggressive if they feel threatened.

hypothermia   A condition in which the body's temperature drops dangerously low because of exposure to cold, wet, or windy weather.

insulation   Material that doesn't conduct electricity or heat, and therefore blocks its flow.

lichen   A living thing that grows on places such as tree trunks or bare ground. Lichens can be yellow, crusty patches or bushy growths.

Lyme disease   A disease that causes a rash, fever, and aches. If left untreated, it can seriously damage the heart, brain, nerves, joints, and eyes.

magnetic North Pole   The spot on the Earth where the north end of a compass needle points. This is because the Earth is like a huge magnet. The ends are called the magnetic North and South Poles, and a weak magnetic current flows between these two ends. Anything magnetic is pulled to line up with the poles.

malaria   A serious disease that is passed on through mosquito bites. Malaria causes chills and fever and can be fatal. If you're visiting an area where malaria is common, you should take anti-malaria drugs before you go.

oxygen   A colorless, odorless gas in the air around us. We need oxygen to breathe, and fires use oxygen to burn.

pollute   To contaminate with poisonous or harmful substances.

signal flare   A device that produces a blaze of light, like a firework without the bang.

stagnant   Water that is still, without any flow or current.

sterile   Completely clean, free from bacteria.

sterilized   Something that has been made sterile, such as a needle.

tarpaulin   A heavy, waterproof sheet, often made of canvas.

tinder   Any fine, soft, or fluffy material that catches fire easily, such as shredded paper, dry moss, or seed heads.

toxic   Something that is harmful because it contains a poisonous substance called a toxin.

venomous   Able to inject a poisonous fluid, called venom, into a victim's body, usually through a bite or a sting.

ventilation   A good flow of air through holes or gaps in a roof or other solid structure. This lets fresh air in and waste gases out.

whiteout   A condition in snowy places where a blizzard, thick clouds, and snow on the ground combine to create a confusing blur of white.

Useful Web Sites

www.wilderness-survival.net
Learn wilderness survival techniques from the U.S. Army training manuals.

www.survivaltopics.com
Read lots of wilderness safety tips and advice.

www.wildwoodsurvival.com
Discover all kinds of survival facts and ideas, including how to prepare for emergencies.

www.wilderness-survival-skills.com
Find out about first aid, signaling for help, and much more. Then test yourself with a quiz.

Index

Answers to survival skills quiz (pages 28–29)

1 c, 2 a, 3 c, 4 b, 5 d, 6 c, 7 b, 8 b, 9 a, 10 d, 11 b, 12 c